The publishers wish to thank the following photographers and photographic agencies for their help in producing this book:

Animals Animals
Carol Cawthra: 14
Breck P. Kent: 43, bottom
Zig Leszczynski: Back cover, top left, and page 24; 35; 39, main picture; 61, bottom
Mark Newman: 17, inset
Charles Palek: 15, top
Michael and Barbara Reed: 32
L. L. T. Rhodes: 58
Leonard Lee Rue III: 19; 20/21, inset; 26; 59
Stouffer Enterprises Inc: Front cover *and* 15, bottom

Ardea (London) Ltd.
Ian Beames: 13, top
Hans and Judy Beste: 60
Kenneth W. Fink: 13, bottom
Ron and Valerie Taylor: 54, inset
Adrian Warren: 18
Caroline Weaver: 27
A. S. Weaving: 10

Barnaby's Picture Library: 28, bottom; 37, top right

David Hosking: Back cover, bottom left, and 37, bottom; 23, top

Eric Hosking: 6; 9; 17, main picture; 28, top; 29; 30; 31; 37, top left; 41; 42

Fernando L. Rodriguez Jimenez: 20/21, main picture

Frank W. Lane
Ron Austing: 56 bottom;
Gösta Håkansson: 61, top right
Marineland of Florida: 57, bottom
Len Robinson: 61, top left
and 50/51, inset; 53, top left, top right and bottom; 54, main picture; 57, top

Oxford Scientific Films Ltd.
Dr. J. A. L. Cooke: 44
Robert W. Mitchell: 33, top and bottom
and back cover, top right, and 48; back cover, bottom right, and 47, top; leading and trailing endpapers; 5, and 50/51, spread; 23, bottom; 34; 38; 39, inset; 40, top and bottom; 43, top; 46; 47, bottom; 49; 55

Photo Aquatics: 56, top

First published 1979 by J. M. Dent and Sons Limited,
Aldine House, Welbeck Street, London
Designed and produced for J. M. Dent and Sons Limited by
Asset Publishing Limited

ISBN 0 460 06896 2 Printed in Great Britain

British Library Cataloguing in Publication Data

Hunters.—(Animal specialists).
1. Predatory animals—Juvenile literature
I. Ellis, Malcolm II. Series
591.5'3 QL758

ISBN 0-460-06896-2

HUNTERS

Editor: Malcolm Ellis

J. M. Dent and Sons Limited
London · Toronto · Melbourne

Contents

Introduction

'The survival of the fittest' is an expression which is frequently used but often not fully understood. In simple terms it means that only the strongest (or most intelligent, or most adaptable) members of an animal population will survive. If they are the ones that survive, they too will be the ones that mate and produce young, thus passing their characteristic of strength to the next generation.

But what happens to those individual animals that are not strong, intelligent or adaptable? If they are very weak or even ill, they may die naturally at an early age. Many of them, however, are killed by other animals, which we call predators—animals that hunt, or prey on, fellow animals. This group, the hunters, includes an enormous number and variety of species, from tiny insects to eagles, tigers and sharks.

Although the ruthless and often bloody activities of the hunters may seem cruel and unjust, they are vital to the balance of nature—that balance which prevents any single species from dominating the Earth. If the hunters did not efficiently weed out the weak and careless members of other animal populations, the weak would survive, reproduce, and pass on their undesirable characteristics, resulting eventually in the death of the species.

The animals who are preyed upon, however, do not let the hunters have things all their own way. Over millions of years of evolution they have developed many methods of escaping their fate. Some, such as the gazelles, have long legs to outrun their pursuers. Others have developed keen senses to detect the approach of a predator—the huge ears of the rabbit, for example, or the sensitive lateral line of a fish. Another widely-used method of defence is camouflage (coloration that blends with the background to hide the animal).

Predators, in turn, have had to refine their hunting techniques and weapons in order to avoid hunger. The big cats, those most graceful and beautiful of killers, rely on a stealthy approach followed by a devastating attack with their sharp teeth and slashing claws. The anglerfish on the sea bed cunningly dangles a lure, in fact the luminous wriggly tip of its dorsal fin, which curves forward to entice prey close enough to be gulped into its mouth. In the air the kestrel hovers over grassland on strong and agile wings until its keen eyesight detects a tiny mouse; then it drops like a thunderbolt to snatch up the prey in its sharp talons. Even tiny creatures have cunning and vicious hunting patterns, as exemplified by the spider, which waits in its intricate, sticky web for prey which it will paralyse with poison.

However efficient the hunter, the chances are that it will itself be preyed upon by a different creature. This pattern of events—one animal preying upon another, which in turn hunts a third, and so on—is called a 'food chain'. In the sea, for example, microscopic animals are eaten by fish; fish are eaten by penguins; penguins may be eaten by leopard seals; leopard seals may fall victim to killer whales.

Left to itself, nature ensures that these food chains remain balanced and unbroken, and that each hunting species has enough to eat without becoming so successful that it destroys its own food supply.

Unfortunately this balance does not take into account the greatest and most powerful hunting animal of all time—modern man.

By killing huge numbers of certain animals, while ignoring or even encouraging others, man has upset the balance of nature on a vast scale. He alone has the power to destroy it, and only he can save his world by sharing it with other animals. If man the hunter destroys all animal life on Earth, 'the survival of the fittest' will become the ultimate irony, for, living as he does at the apex of the food chain, he cannot survive alone.

Opposite: It is usually lionesses that make the kills to feed the pride. From the age of six months, the lion cubs join in the hunt and learn from their mothers.

The Big Carnivores

The name 'carnivore' literally means 'flesh-eater' and is normally applied to mammals which devour the flesh of other animals, which they themselves have usually hunted and killed.

Undoubtedly the most spectacular of the carnivores are the big cats; powerful, often solitary, hunters, they stalk their prey silently or lie in wait for it. They possess two large canine teeth in each jaw for seizing the prey, while their sharp cheek teeth cut rather than chew the flesh into chunks to be swallowed. Their claws are retractile, which means they can be drawn back under folds of skin on the toes so that they do not scrape on the ground and become blunt, but are sharp when extended to strike down prey or to climb trees.

Perhaps the best known of the big cats is, of course, the lion. It lives mainly on the grasslands of Africa, with a small and extremely rare population in the Gir Forest of India. Lions live in groups, called prides, and usually hunt together. In Africa, the lion's prey includes many large grazing animals, especially wildebeest (gnu) and zebra, but also gazelles, impala, giraffe and warthog.

Lions usually hunt at dawn or dusk. In larger prides, the lionesses do most of the hunting, but the males always eat first. A typical hunt begins with one or two lionesses walking in full view towards a herd of grazing animals, such as zebra. At the same time, other lionesses advance unseen from behind. The herd panics at the sight of the approaching lions, turns, and rushes straight into the ambush.

The hidden lionesses charge suddenly, reaching a speed of up to 56 kmph. They kill by leaping at the victim's neck, striking it with their powerful forepaws and pulling the animal to the ground, their teeth biting its throat until the creature quickly suffocates. With smaller prey such as antelopes, the lion leaps on to the animal's hindquarters and its weight breaks the victim's back.

Four out of five hunts, however, are unsuccessful, because the prey is too swift and the lion lacks the speed and stamina for a long chase.

Mainly a nocturnal and solitary hunter, the tiger can be bigger than the largest lion. This magnificent cat is immensely strong and can bring down a large deer with one blow from a forepaw. It preys mostly on hoofed animals such as deer, the gaur (largest of all wild cattle), buffalo, pigs, and sometimes elephant calves and domestic cattle. The tiger's diet also includes birds, reptiles and even frogs and fish. It is a good swimmer, but though able to climb, seldom does. Sometimes it lies in wait for prey near a water-hole or track, concealed among thick vegetation where its black-striped coat camouflages it well against the light and shade of the forest.

The tiger will stalk its prey to within 9 to 24 m, then suddenly charge from behind, topple it with a blow from a forepaw and, gripping with its claws, drag the victim to the ground. Large prey is suffocated as the tiger bites its throat; smaller prey is killed by a bite in the back of the neck. The tiger, like the lion, lacks stamina for a long chase.

The tiger often drags a kill to a secluded spot to eat it. It may consume 18 to 22 kg of meat straight away, then hide the remains and return later for another meal, leaving only the large bones.

The tiger once ranged from Turkey all the way across Asia to China. Now the main population is restricted to India and South-East Asia. The Siberian tiger—a truly magnificent beast and the biggest cat in the world—is now very rare and confined to remote mountainous regions.

Another mainly nocturnal and solitary predator is the leopard. Although smaller than the lion and tiger, weight for weight the leopard's strength and agility is greater. The leopard, or panther as it is sometimes called, ranges throughout much of

Opposite: The leopard often drags its prey, which may weigh more than itself, up a tree to eat it undisturbed by other hunters or scavengers.

Opposite, top: The cheetah is justly famous among animal hunters for its unrivalled speed. Cheetahs have been domesticated and used for sport, like greyhounds.

Opposite, bottom: The snow leopard's warm coat helps to insulate it from the cold of its Himalayan home, where it preys on mountain goats and other small animals. It is in turn preyed upon by man for the sake of its fur.

Africa and Asia, and lives in both tropical forest and open wooded country.

Perhaps the most stealthy of the big cats, the leopard is well camouflaged by its coat which is decorated with clusters or rosettes of black spots. It hunts small antelopes, bush pigs, monkeys, rodents and birds, and also tends to be a scavenger. It stalks its prey silently and then suddenly leaps on to it: often the leopard springs from a branch above the victim. It crushes the necks of small animals and mauls the hindquarters of larger ones before seizing the throat. The kill is dragged under cover so that the leopard can feed undisturbed. Being an excellent climber, it often carries a carcass up a tree, out of reach of scavengers such as jackals and hyenas: it is capable of carrying a carcass twice its own weight.

Living in the mountainous regions of the Himalayas and Mongolia is the rare snow leopard. The only truly alpine cat, it is found at altitudes of up to 6,100 m. It is about the same size as the lowland leopard but has longer and thicker fur, which is light grey-brown in colour, with blurred black rosettes. The snow leopard shelters at night in a rocky den and emerges during the day to hunt wild mountain sheep, goats and yak calves, as well as small mammals and birds. As there are no trees at high altitudes from which it can leap, it hunts by stalking its prey.

Heavier than all the big cats except the lion and tiger is the jaguar. It lives in Central and South America, where it inhabits tropical rain forests, and also grasslands and desert areas, though there it is more rare.

This cat looks rather like a stockily-built, short-legged leopard, but the black rosettes which adorn its coat have a central spot, unlike those of the leopard. The black jaguar, a dark form of this big cat, can be found in dense, humid forests, just as the black leopard or panther occurs in the wetter forests of Asia.

The jaguar is a powerful jumper and swims well; it can climb trees, but does not have the agility of the leopard. The jaguar hunts mostly at night for animals such as tapir, deer and agoutis, but especially peccaries—a kind of forest pig. It lies in wait, watching peccary herds for the opportunity to seize any straggler, and hides along river banks waiting for animals to come to drink. It will scoop fish out of the water with a forepaw. Birds are also included in the jaguar's diet.

America is also the home of the puma, also known as the mountain lion or cougar. This adaptable cat lives in a variety of habitats, from mountains and wooded hillsides to jungles and deserts. It has been shot, poisoned and trapped for many years because of the damage it causes among domestic stock, and now occurs only in more remote regions.

In the mountains above the treeline, the puma hunts by day, preying mostly on deer, wild sheep and rodents. Lowland pumas, which are smaller than those of the mountains, are mainly nocturnal hunters. Like some of the other big cats, the puma often hides the remains of a kill and returns later for another meal.

The last of the big cats is the cheetah. A leanly-built, long-legged predator, it is unique in being the only member of the cat family with non-retractile claws. This cat is at home on the grasslands and semi-desert areas of Africa, but there its numbers are dwindling and it has all but disappeared from most of its former range in south-west Asia.

The cheetah lives in pairs or small family groups and hunts during the day, usually in the early morning and late afternoon. It preys on small hoofed animals, such as gazelles and impala, but also on hares and birds, and on rare occasions takes animals as large as wildebeest.

The fastest animal on four legs, the cheetah can reach speeds of about 112 kmph. It can maintain this speed for about 500 m but lacks stamina for a longer chase. It will nearly always overtake a young fawn, but the swifter adult deer often escape.

Before the sprint, the cheetah walks

slowly towards its prey—a herd of gazelles, for example—and, as they panic and flee, it selects one individual and bounds after it in a sudden burst of speed. The victim is knocked down by a blow from a forepaw and its throat seized in a suffocating grip.

A family of cheetahs quickly devour their kill, as any delay gives the lion and hyenas the opportunity to rob them of it. Vultures can sometimes drive a single cheetah from its kill. In fact, the cheetah loses a large number of kills to other animals. Young cheetahs are preyed on by the lion, leopard and hyenas.

There are several big predators to be found among the ranks of the dog family. Dogs are generally good runners and have the stamina to pursue their prey for considerable distances, hunting mainly by scent; they also have keen hearing and sight. They possess sharp teeth and strong jaws for holding prey, biting, tearing the flesh and crushing bones. All dogs

have non-retractile claws. Unlike many of the big cats which are solitary, dogs often live and hunt in packs.

Most breeds of domestic dogs which we keep today as pets were believed to have descended from the wolf and perhaps the jackal. More recently, though, it has been suggested that the ancestor of most domestic dogs may have been a wild dog of a kind which has long been extinct.

The dingo was domesticated in Asia and taken to Australia thousands of years ago where it quickly reverted to its wild ways and was one of the main causes of the decline or extinction of many Australian marsupials. It was probably competition with the dingo which caused the thylacine to disappear from the Australian mainland. Known also, though misleadingly, as the Tasmanian wolf or tiger, the thylacine may still survive on Tasmania, which the dingo never reached.

Once widespread over Europe, much of Asia and North America, the wolf has been persecuted for centuries and now survives only in remote areas. Today when we think of the wolf, we probably picture it roaming the North American Arctic tundra, hunting in packs for the caribou (the wild North American reindeer). In the far north the wolf sometimes has a white coat throughout the year and may be known as the white or polar wolf. Others may be called grey wolves or timber wolves. Despite the different names, they are not entirely separate kinds of wolf, but merely variations of the one species. Wolves from different parts of North America, Asia and Europe have their own racial characteristics; for example in Florida, USA, the wolf may be black.

The pack is frequently a family group of about ten animals. However, during the migrations of herds of hoofed animals, wolf packs often combine in mass hunting attacks. Their biggest prey on the tundra is the musk ox. They also hunt moose (elk) and other deer, as well as smaller animals, including rodents such as lemmings, and even eat carrion. Wolves rarely hide the remains of a kill and must hunt throughout the winter or starve.

When prey such as a herd of caribou is sighted, a wolf pack will usually watch for a calf or weak adult which is unable to keep up with the others. Members of the pack take turns to lead the chase, until eventually the victim becomes exhausted and is overtaken and killed.

In the coastal marshlands of south-eastern USA lives the red wolf. Although it feeds mainly on rodents, it is poisoned as a suspected killer of domestic stock and its future is greatly endangered. The grasslands of South America are the home of the long-legged maned wolf. A shy, mainly solitary and nocturnal animal, its diet consists mostly of small mammals, but also birds, reptiles, insects and even fruit.

Smaller than the wolves is the coyote which, despite considerable persecution, is widespread on the grasslands of Central and North America. The coyote usually hunts alone; after

Below: African hunting dogs squabble over a kill, probably a young or weak animal snatched from the herd.

Left: The timber wolf was once common in Europe but it is now found mainly in Canada and Alaska, where it follows the migrations of its chief prey, the caribou.

Below: The name of the coyote is synonymous with cunning, and this is displayed in its hunting methods.

spending the day hidden among rocks or under cover, it emerges at night to search for its prey, which consists mainly of small animals. Occasionally it forms packs, which will attack deer and weakened bison (sometimes called buffalo).

The dhole—Indian or Asiatic wild dog—lives in packs. Deer are the main prey, but wild pigs, buffalo, and all manner of other animals are also hunted. These dogs possess great stamina and follow their prey by scent over long distances, pursuing it relentlessly until it comes within view and is eventually dragged down and killed. A dhole pack is capable of driving a tiger or leopard from its kill and stealing the carcass.

One of the most efficient and feared African predators is the African or Cape hunting dog. It ranges widely over the open plains in packs, which prey on gazelles, wildebeest and zebra, or any other animals which can be overpowered.

Hunting usually at dawn or just before dusk, a pack of dogs will approach a grazing herd and select an individual which is too young or weak to keep up with the others as they flee in alarm. The dogs pursue it relentlessly, ignoring the rest of the herd. The chase may continue for a considerable distance until the victim is exhausted; then the dogs bring it down and tear it to pieces.

After the kill has been made, the hunting dogs gorge themselves, rapidly swallowing chunks of meat before hyenas have time to gather and drive them from their spoils. Members of the dog pack which arrive too late are fed on food regurgitated by others. The dogs take turns to hunt and those which stay behind to guard the pups are fed by regurgitation when the pack returns.

Dog-like in appearance, but in fact more closely related to cats, are the hyenas. There are three kinds—the spotted hyena, brown hyena and striped hyena. The first two kinds live only in Africa, while the striped hyena ranges from north-east Africa through south-west Asia to India.

Because their hindlegs are shorter and less muscular than their front legs, hyenas have a very characteristic stance, with high shoulders and the back sloping down to the hindquarters. Their jaws are probably the most powerful of all mammals' in relation to their size, and their massive teeth are capable of crushing the heaviest of bones.

Hyenas are principally scavengers and feed on carcasses and carrion. In Africa, they frequently scavenge lions' kills; the hyenas gather nearby while the lions have their fill, and later move in to finish off the remains of the carcass. Packs of hyenas sometimes drive lions, cheetahs and African hunting dogs from their kills.

The spotted hyena has been found to be a predator in its own right. It hunts at night in packs of up to thirty, preying mainly on wildebeest, zebra and gazelles. It will also kill very young or very old lions. Lions, however, are not dominated by hyenas, and often drive hyenas away from their own kills.

The African plains are also frequented by jackals. The commonest and most widespread is the black-backed jackal. It will tackle anything it can reasonably hope to overcome, and will often congregate in packs to follow hunting lions in the hope of picking up some carrion. In its turn, the jackal is preyed upon by the leopard and even large pythons.

There are four kinds of jackal, three of which are confined to Africa; but the fourth, known in Africa as the golden jackal, also occurs in south-east Europe and southern Asia, including India, and may also be called the Asiatic jackal. Jackals live alone, in pairs, or in small packs. They usually spend their days lying up in thickets or amongst undergrowth, and venture out at night in search of food.

Jackals are slightly built animals, and when trotting lightly along they give the impression of being smaller than a domestic collie. They look very dog-like; in fact they are intermediate between wolves and foxes, and show traits of both.

Opposite: Although the hyena is widely despised as a cowardly scavenger, in fact it often joins in marauding groups to kill prey, using its powerful jaws (inset).

Smaller Predators

Since the disappearance of the lynx, bear and wolf from Britain and much of Europe, the only remaining carnivore of any size still commonly found in this country is the much-abused red fox—which survives despite considerable persecution by human beings, who ought to value it. The fox deserves our support since it is an important controller of the small animals that man likes to call vermin. It is not a specialist feeder and will take just about anything it can find. As well as being a hunter, it is also a confirmed scavenger—forever scouring and cleaning up the countryside, and, more recently, our towns as well. It is not clean in its own habits, however, and the location of its earth is usually betrayed by the rubbish around it and an unmistakable odour.

The fox displays its legendary cleverness in several ways; for example, it will bury eggs when in plentiful supply, digging them up later when food is scarce. Recent evidence that the fox is not a serious threat to sheep and lambs supports what naturalists have felt for a long time: that the fox does more good than harm to the environment. If the fox ravages chicken-runs, as it certainly will if given the chance, the farmer has only himself to blame for not protecting his livelihood better. In other parts of the world foxes are persecuted for different reasons, even if they do no damage to domestic animals: the Arctic fox in particular, with its beautiful, thick, silvery coat, is a prime quarry for fur-trappers in Canada.

One fox which seldom comes into conflict with man is the exquisite little fennec fox, an inhabitant of the suffocatingly hot deserts of North Africa and Arabia. The extremely high daytime temperatures mean that the fennec fox has little alternative but to stay in its shady, cool burrow. It usually remains there until sunset, and then emerges to hunt for lizards, insects, birds and their eggs, and small desert rodents.

Like their larger relatives, the smaller wild cats have all the characteristics to make them the élite predators: with their keen eyesight, sharp claws, and graceful stealth, they are at once terrible and beautiful. Many of them are adorned with the superb coats which are so coveted by the big fashion houses and by rich women everywhere. Consequently many smaller cats are rare, even endangered.

The ocelot in particular is currently suffering greatly from the persecution of trappers. Its buffish coat, covered in large spots, helps to render it almost invisible in the forests of Central and South America. With the help of this camouflage it hunts its prey at dusk or by night—though sometimes in the day. In common with other cats its acute hearing helps it to locate its prey in the dimly-lit jungle. Although at home in the treetops it usually hunts on the jungle floor. The ocelot's diet consists of animals as large as small deer, pigs and boa snakes, although medium-sized rodents form the major part.

In Africa, the serval lives in more

Opposite: Like most of the cat family, the ocelot is an expert climber, but it usually hunts its prey on the forest floor.

Below: One of the most familiar of British animal predators, the fox has adapted to a life close to humans, and often lives and hunts in city suburbs.

open country. While it does from time to time venture into wooded areas, the serval's plainer-coloured coat is indicative of an animal at home in sandy and grassy land. Lightly built with long limbs, it is ideally suited to chasing prey in the open, and is probably happiest when in pursuit of free-running quarry such as hares and duikers (small antelopes).

One hunter which should not be overlooked, despite its familiar status as a pet, is the domestic cat. It has changed surprisingly little from a wild animal, and constantly provides a splendid illustration of the ways in which wild cats live and hunt. To watch a domestic cat stalking a bird across a lawn, or patiently lying in wait for an unsuspecting vole, is not so different to watching a lion on the African plains.

It is tempting—though erroneous—to think of the domestic tabby cat as a descendant of the superficially similar European wild cat, which is still to be found in remote parts of the Scottish highlands, and other areas of Europe and Asia. The European wild cat is a different animal altogether—virtually untameable, savage and ruthless. Like most other cats it is a lone hunter since only in this way can it be sure of the absolute silence it needs for an ambush, or the stealthy stalking which is, as with the domestic cat, decisively ended by a silent pounce.

Grouse, rodents and hares form the bulk of the wild cat's diet but anything of reasonable size encountered on its twilight and nocturnal hunting expeditions is sure to be tackled.

Otters are another group of carnivores, which achieve their greatest hunting success in a different element—water. Very much aquatic hunters, the majority of otter species prefer fresh water, although the common or Eurasian otter is one of several which will happily take to coastal living if necessary. The sea otter of the north Pacific coasts is exclusively marine.

The otter is superbly adapted for fast and agile swimming. Its coat is

Left: The serval stalks its prey over grassland, camouflaged by its colouring. Inset: The otter's streamlined agility makes him an efficient hunter in water.

thick and totally waterproof, and trapped within the soft undercoat is a layer of air which keeps the animal warm and buoyant. It swims by strong strokes of its powerful hind limbs, which have webbed toes, and by waving its muscular tail. The otter is most noted as a catcher of fish—which it pursues relentlessly, following every twist and turn of its prey until the doomed victim is caught. To help the otter locate its prey in murky waters it has a magnificent set of long, tough whiskers, which are sensitive to the slightest water turbulence caused by potential prey.

Closely related to the otter, and often more successful in areas where they compete for food, is the mink. The mink is now widespread throughout Britain, following innumerable escapes from mink farms where it is kept and bred for its valuable coat. Much the same has happened in Europe, where the introduced North American mink has largely displaced the native European species.

The mink generally lives in wooded country near water. It is an expert swimmer and is perfectly equipped to catch fish and waterfowl—especially their young—but it is also thoroughly at home on dry land, covering wide areas on nightly searches for rodents and birds. It displays all the tenacity and ferocity which are characteristic of the mustelids—the group of animals which includes otters, badgers, weasels, and skunks. This group contains some of nature's fiercest fighters and most successful predators.

A familiar mustelid is the stoat, somewhat larger than the weasel, with which it is often confused; the stoat has a longer tail with a distinctive black tip.

Both the stoat and weasel are formidable hunters of small animals such as rodents and birds, and are never far from farms, but the stoat's preferred food is the rabbit, and it keeps a valuable check on rabbit populations. The stoat occurs over a wide variety of habitats, hunting in woods, farmland, under hedges and on riverbanks.

In the far north of its range, the stoat grows a white coat during the autumn, beneath its normal reddish-brown one. When it gets very cold, the brown hairs drop out in a matter of days leaving the animal perfectly camouflaged in its snowy home. This pure white coat, with the black tail-tip which is never lost, forms the valuable fur 'ermine' often used to edge royal robes.

Closely related to the mustelids, the mongoose inevitably owes much of its fame to Rudyard Kipling's story *Rikki-Tikki-Tavi*, which accurately portrays the character and tenacity of these small carnivores. Snakes, while certainly a major part of their diet, are by no means all they eat; rats are also favoured. Both are killed by a quick rush and fierce, uninhibited biting from the very sharp teeth and strong jaws of the mongoose. Eggs are another favourite food.

Over much of the tropical and subtropical Old World, mongooses replace the weasels as the principal small carnivore and can be found wherever there is thick ground cover.

One of the rarest of hunters, and not as ferocious as its name suggests, the Tasmanian devil is found only in the rugged and remote parts of Tasmania. It has been mercilessly eradicated from areas of human settlement because of its raids on domestic fowl and young lambs. It kills rats, mice and other small animals, as well as wallabies, small kangaroos, reptiles and birds. The devil acquired its name because of its black fur, evil expression, aggressive behaviour and strange snarl. The Tasmanian devil is one of Australia's many marsupials—a group of animals whose young are initially reared in a pouch on the mother's body.

The shrew pictured here lives mostly on insects and is only about 7 cm long from nose to tail-tip. For its size, however, the shrew is just about the fiercest animal of all, habitually attacking and eating not only insects but any other small animal it chances to encounter on its regular hunting trips.

Opposite, top: Weight for weight, the common shrew must be one of the fiercest of hunters. Here it makes a meal of a juicy earthworm.

Opposite, bottom: With its needle-sharp teeth, a weasel despatches its harvest mouse prey. It will take on larger animals such as rabbits.

Shrews are quite simply eating machines: every 24 hours they have to eat their own weight in food just to survive. They need to consume a large amount of food because they use up so much energy in hunting, and because very small mammals lose heat quickly and soon 'burn up' their food intake.

Shrews are as intolerant of each other as they are of other animals, and should one encounter another in its territory—which might be only a few square metres—they will argue violently. Not surprisingly, they do not live long, wearing themselves out in less than two years and suffering heavy predation from birds of prey.

Winged Hunters

When we think of winged hunters we usually think first of those popularly known as birds of prey, or raptors. Apart from the many species of owl, there are more than 270 other different birds of prey. This includes the eagles, buzzards, kites, harriers, hawks and falcons, the ospreys and the secretary birds. It also includes the vultures, which are primarily scavengers living on carrion.

A typical bird of prey has a sharply hooked beak, and strong legs and feet, armed with sharp, curved claws, sometimes called talons. It is the clawed feet (or talons) that are most often used to seize and kill its prey; it may also use the beak to bite at the base of the victim's skull, and, when the victim is dead, to tear from the carcass pieces of flesh which are then swallowed.

One of the most familiar and widespread of the eagles is the golden eagle, a splendid flier which can soar effortlessly for hours. The golden eagle is proficient at killing mammals and birds. The mammals generally range up to the size of a hare. The large golden eagles in Asia, however, may even take wolves and have been known to kill fairly large deer. Gamebirds such as grouse may also form a considerable part of a golden eagle's food.

Some eagles are accused of killing lambs and other domestic stock. Although, very rarely, lambs of up to three weeks old are killed, the farmer should consider the numbers of harmful rabbits and other large rodents, as well as potential predators like young foxes, that may be killed by the eagles. Certainly, the golden eagle is not adverse to eating dead animals, both domestic and wild.

The largest and most powerful eagle is the harpy eagle. This magnificent bird lives high among the giant forest trees of tropical Central and South America. It seldom soars in the open sky, but keeps close to the treetops, using strong, deep wingbeats and short, swift glides to swoop on its prey: monkeys feeding in the treetops on fruit; sloths, snatched with a remarkable sideways manoeuvre; the tamandua, a tree-living anteater; and tree porcupines, are on this eagle's menu, as are macaws, the large colourful parrots.

Occasionally the harpy eagle descends from its lofty home to the forest floor to snatch large rodents called agoutis, and even small peccaries—wild pigs. Aided by its short, broad wings and the vice-like grip of its feet, the harpy is well able to lift quite heavy prey almost vertically.

Only a little smaller than the harpy eagle, but, if anything, looking even more fierce, is the monkey-eating eagle. Found only on a few of the Philippine Islands, its existence is gravely endangered by the felling of its forest habitat, and by a local fashion for stuffed specimens as trophies.

Its main food is flying lemurs, but true to its name it also kills monkeys; other prey includes flying squirrels, tree squirrels, and probably fairly large birds like hornbills.

Among the most accomplished fliers are the larger falcons, and none more so than the peregrine. This bird is absolutely exhilarating to watch in flight. It possesses supreme skill and grace and is capable of tremendous speed combined with hairbreadth accuracy. The peregrine falcon's prowess as a hunter derives particularly from its slanting dive, called the 'stoop'. With wings almost closed, the bird rockets earthwards, often striking its feathered quarry dead in the air with a hind claw, or seizing it in a foot and bringing it to the ground.

The speed of the peregrine's stoop is the subject of wildly differing estimates: often reckoned at 240 to 320 kmph, recent evidence suggests it may even achieve 440 kmph. Whatever the truth, peregrines regularly strike down small finches, and some take birds up to the size of ducks and small geese. Other medium-sized birds such as red grouse and pigeons—especially the rock dove—are favourites.

Opposite: Surprised by the photographer, a long-eared owl assumes its threat posture, daring anyone to steal its prey.

Small, long-winged and exceedingly fast, the hobbies are falcons which feed mostly on flying insects, but will also take some small birds, including swifts, in flight. Small birds are also taken in flight by the merlin, another small falcon.

The kestrel, the commonest falcon in Britain and Europe, also lives in parts of Africa and Asia; like the American kestrel (often misleadingly called the American sparrowhawk) it is able to hover with fanned wings. This is a good way to survey patches of long grass which offer refuge to the mice, voles and insects which are the kestrel's most common prey.

Quick, dashing fliers, the true sparrowhawks' noticeably rounded wings and fairly long tail give them not only the speed but the control that is necessary to twist and turn when hunting in woodland. These medium-sized hawks kill mainly other birds, though some smaller sparrowhawks take many insects; and the largest—the goshawk, at 46 to 60 cm—is capable of killing mammals as big as a rabbit.

The national bird of the USA, the bald eagle, eats mostly fish. A few of these it catches alive but most are found dead or dying. This includes salmon brought to the water's edge and partly eaten by bears.

The bald eagle is not a true eagle but one of several fish or sea eagles, which include some of the largest and finest of all birds of prey. They live mostly by rivers, lakes and the sea coast, as does that most skilful hunter of fish, the osprey.

In common with fish or sea eagles, this expert fisher likes to sit on a dead tree, a post projecting from the water, or perhaps a rock, from where, with slow purposeful strokes of its long wings, it flies often in circles or figures-of-eight, watching carefully for unwary fish swimming close to the surface. When such quarry is spotted, the osprey may dive directly on to the fish, or alight relatively gently and virtually pluck the fish from the water.

On occasions there is a more spectacular encounter—the osprey, on sighting a fish, will hover briefly with fanned wings and legs dangling below. Then, with the head thrust well forward, the wings held above the back and the tail spread, it will throw out its feet and plunge into the water.

The osprey has specially adapted feet: the four toes of each foot are roughly the same length and the outer front toe can be turned back; more importantly, the underside of each toe has short, spine-like scales, which with the long needle-sharp claws make the feet ideally equipped to grasp slippery, wriggling fish up to 2 kg.

The secretary bird is unique, for it is the only bird of prey with long stilt-like legs. Its name originates from a reputed likeness between its long crest feathers and the old-fashioned quill pens which secretaries and clerks used to place behind the ear.

Although fossil remains of the secre-

Below: Symbol of America, the bald eagle lives mostly on fish, and is more of a scavenger than a killer.

tary bird have been found in France, it lives today only in Africa, south of the Sahara. It favours open country with fairly short grass, scattered bushes, or sometimes thicker vegetation.

Pairs and family parties often hunt together; walking with long, measured strides, they may cover 32 km or more a day. The normal gait is interspersed with quick stamping steps which have the effect of flushing out likely prey. From time to time the secretary bird will make a dart to one side, or open its wings and run a few paces in pursuit of some small creature. This is usually taken with a quick thrust of the head and speedily swallowed.

The main prey is small rodents like mice and rats, but animals up to the size of a young hare are killed. Birds, particularly young ones, eggs, lizards and insects also figure prominently in their diet. One secretary bird's stomach was found to contain locusts, a chameleon, an adder, a tortoise, frogs, a quail, rats and other remains.

Large prey is dispatched by using a foot to stamp on it. After each stamp, the secretary bird steps back a pace or so, then circles the victim, before jumping in to deliver another hammer-blow. This strategy continues until the bird is satisfied that the creature is dead. In this way, the secretary bird attacks snakes, including poisonous species, using its outstretched wings to protect the body from any bites.

When day gives way to night, the place of the daytime (diurnal) birds of prey is taken by a variety of owls. Well adapted for night-time (nocturnal) hunting, they possess large, sensitive eyes and exceptionally acute hearing, and usually have soft, velvety plumage which enables them to move and strike with the utmost silence.

There are about 130 species of owl in the world, and they occur in most places, Antarctica being a notable exception. The elf owl is the smallest; like the pygmy falcons, it is scarcely bigger than a sparrow and generally eats insects. A wide variety of live prey is taken by owls. In Africa there are three fishing owls which have feet similar to the osprey's. They are little-known owls, but evidence suggests their main prey is freshwater fish. Asian fishing owls also eat fish, but consume many other aquatic creatures, as well as birds and mammals. The great eagle owl, nearly as big as a golden eagle, is capable of killing quite large animals, as are others such as the American great horned owl.

The widely distributed barn owl is easily recognized by its fairly plain white and buff plumage, heart-shaped face and long, slender legs. This owl frequently spends the day sitting quietly inside a farm building or perhaps a church steeple, from where at dusk it sets off to hunt.

Not all owls are exclusively night birds; many hunt at dusk and dawn, and several, such as the little owl, hunt regularly during the day.

Below: The secretary bird's appearance—like a Victorian clerk with his pens tucked behind his ears—earned him his name.

A formidable predator, the snowy owl—although well able to strike down geese and hares—relies for food mostly on lemmings, small rodents which are subject to regular peaks or 'explosions' in their populations. At such times, the snowy owl may lay as many as 14 eggs, confident in the knowledge that there will be sufficient food to feed a large brood.

Penguins, cormorants and darters (the last are also known as snakebirds or anhingas) are very active hunters. These water birds all take live prey, mostly fish, which is also the food of the pelicans. These birds have a huge beak with an enormous pouch which is used as a most effective fishing net.

Pelicans are highly sociable and commonly form fishing parties. When they find a shoal of fish, the pelicans swim towards the shore in an arc formation, flapping their wings and making quite a commotion, which has the effect of driving the fish into the shallows, where they can easily be scooped up. Not only is the American brown pelican the smallest pelican, but, unlike the rest of the family, it is much more a seabird, with a vastly different way of fishing. The brown pelican plunges into the water, often from a considerable height and with a resounding splash, in the manner of gannets as they dive for fish.

By contrast, herons usually stand alone and motionless at the water's edge, or in shallows, where they wait patiently for their fish prey to swim within striking distance of their spear-like beaks. The grey or common heron can frequently be observed in many parts of the Old World hunting in this fashion, and in America the great blue heron does the same.

In the southern USA, some green herons have become quite ingenious and learned to collect scraps of bread, place them in water and catch the fish which come to eat. A young heron was seen to use a feather successfully as a lure.

The black heron, which lives in Africa, has developed a remarkable hunting method: it stands motionless in shallow water, with its wings

brought forward and spread in an umbrella-like way. One explanation for this strange behaviour is that the patch of shade created by the wings acts as a false refuge and lures fish within range of the bird's lethal beak. A more simple answer is that reflections from the sunlit water are cut out by the wings, making it far easier for the heron to spot its prey.

The kingfishers, todies, motmots, bee-eaters and rollers, together with the jacamars, could well be termed the 'colourful killers'. Renowned for their brilliant colours, they are all carnivorous, eating other living creatures.

Although there are over 80 different kingfishers, only the common kingfisher is widespread in Britain and Europe; it also occurs in Africa and Asia, including India, and eastwards to the Solomon Islands. It frequently sits on a branch overhanging a river or stream and, on sighting a fish, plunges headlong into the water as straight as an arrow. It catches the fish, not as might be supposed by stabbing, but simply by grasping it in its long, pointed beak. The bird then pivots and, by using the buoyancy of its body and

Opposite, top: The black heron's trick of shading the water may help to cut out reflections from the water surface when hunting.

Opposite, bottom: The dagger-like bill of a heron is ideally designed for stabbing prey, such as this big water rat.

Left: A streak of blue is as much as one usually sees of the shy kingfisher, darting upriver in search of fish prey.

flapping its wings, bounces back to the surface, leaving the water on the downstroke of the wings. The whole action, from the time the kingfisher dives to the time it returns to the perch, may take less than a second.

With the fish held firmly in its beak, and using deft sideways sweeps, the kingfisher proceeds to beat the fish vigorously and repeatedly against the perch to kill it. The fish is then swallowed head first, ensuring that it slides down smoothly and that no fins or spines stick in the bird's throat.

The majority of kingfishers, however, rarely eat fish; indeed, many live some way from water. Most catch insects, lizards and other small creatures. Two of the more widespread species are the white-breasted and white-collared kingfishers. The slightly smaller sacred kingfisher is common in Australia and is the only kingfisher which lives in New Zealand.

The kookaburra is large and fairly drab by kingfisher standards. Its raucous cries—often uttered in chorus—are among Australia's most characteristic sounds and are responsible for this bird's several nicknames, the most familiar being 'laughing jackass'. It takes a wide variety of prey and has quite a reputation as a snake-killer. As all kingfishers possess relatively small, weak feet, the kookaburra has to rely upon its beak when dealing with snakes.

Perhaps even more colourful than the kingfishers, the bee-eaters are a strictly Old World family with one, the Australian bee-eater, commonly called the rainbow-bird. The European bee-eater's food has been carefully analysed, and shown to be mostly honey-bee workers and drones. Experiments have proved that the bird

Right: The call of the kookaburra sounds like manic laughter, hence its other name of 'laughing jackass'.

is able to discriminate between the stinging worker bees and similar, but non-stinging, drones.

When it snaps up a stinging worker in flight, the bee-eater, on its return to its perch, uses a flick of the beak to transfer its grip closer to the sting at the tip of the abdomen. Several bouts of beating and rubbing against the perch cause the bee to discharge its venom, then, following more sharp blows, the bee is tossed up and swallowed.

Although the carmine bee-eater takes many bees and wasps, including the big carpenter bee, it is especially adept at finding locusts and grasshoppers. Just as the cattle egret follows domestic animals, elephant and buffalo to snap up the numerous insects and small creatures which are disturbed by the animals as they move about the African plains, so the carmine bee-eater hunts in association with other animals. Often it chooses to ride on the back of an Abdim's stork or kori bustard, and from this most convenient moving perch, swoops down to snap up insects which are flushed up by the feet of the bigger birds.

Together with the secretary bird, black kite, grasshopper buzzard, and rollers, the carmine bee-eater is attracted to bush fires, where it feasts on the fleeing insects. It nests in burrows in riverbanks and similar sites. Although no nesting material as such is used, the eggs and later the nestlings become cushioned on a layer of discarded insect remains. The adult bee-eaters also regurgitate blackish pellets about 2·5 cm long which are composed of the indigestible parts of insects. These soon dry and crumble and so add to the carpet of debris.

Not only the so-called birds of prey are winged hunters. Among smaller carnivorous birds, shrikes are confirmed hunters. Bold and aggressive, they have strong, hooked beaks often with a sharp 'tooth', and also have powerful legs and feet. In several respects they resemble miniature birds of prey, albeit, in the case of many tropical shrikes, very colourful ones.

Some of these birds catch only insects, but others take a variety of small creatures, including other birds and mammals, as well. Small prey is usually carried in the beak but larger items may be held in the feet. Many shrikes wedge their prey in the fork of a branch or impale it on a thorn or other sharp object, including, sometimes, barbed wire. A shrike may use a site repeatedly and assemble a collection of surplus food which is left uneaten and forms what is called a 'larder'. This gruesome habit has led to the popular name 'butcher bird' being given to these shrikes.

This nickname is frequently applied to the red-backed shrike. Like other shrikes it locates much of its prey from an observation point, often at the top of an isolated bush. Frequently this is a spiky gorse or thorn bush, which also proves ideal as a 'larder'. The red-backed shrike takes many beetles and bees, as well as other insects, frogs, lizards and small mammals, especially rodents. Birds, their nestlings, and those which have recently left the nest are killed, including chicks of pheasants and partridges.

Apart from swooping down to take prey on the ground, this shrike sometimes hovers like a kestrel, and will occasionally fly rapidly along a hedge or into thick cover in an attempt to flush out prey, as does a sparrowhawk.

The great grey shrike is known as the northern shrike in North America, which is one of four continents where it occurs. It is bigger and stronger than the red-backed shrike and takes many

Left: Common in warm lands, the carmine bee-eater is a sociable bird that may gather in huge colonies to nest and hunt.

more birds, occasionally killing those as big as a thrush.

A familiar sight in open woodland and some parks and gardens in Europe during the summer is the spotted flycatcher. This small sober-coloured bird usually sits rather upright on a post, stump, or exposed bare branch and sallies forth to snap up passing insects. Because it depends on flying prey, the spotted flycatcher has difficulty hunting effectively during rainy weather and obviously cannot remain in Europe through the winter.

A large number of different flycatchers, some of them very brightly coloured, live in subtropical and tropical regions where seasonal changes are less pronounced, and where there is a wide range of flying insects throughout the year. Among many which hunt insects in typical flycatcher fashion are the paradise flycatchers of Africa and Asia; others, like the wattle-eye flycatchers, search for insects on leaves and branches in a similar way to many warblers and tits.

Flycatchers have large heads and broad, flattened beaks, usually with bristles at the base which help to direct insects snapped out of the air—often with an audible click of the beak—into the wide gape. The American flycatchers, of which there are about 362 different species with names like kingbird, phoebe, pewee, kiskadee and tyrant, are often known collectively as tyrant flycatchers.

The great crested flycatcher, as well as hunting on the wing, sometimes drops down to the ground to seize insects. It also takes large numbers of caterpillars and some wild berries when these are in season. The scissor-tailed and swallow-tailed flycatchers have long, deeply forked tails which stream out as they dash after insects.

Insects are the main food of many other small birds, including the robin. Even the tiny hummingbirds supplement their diet of nectar with minute insects. Many birds include insects in their diet at the onset of breeding or when feeding their young. Some finches, and other birds which as adults eat little else but seed, feed their newly-hatched young only insects.

The only mammals which truly fly, as opposed to glide, are the bats. There are about 900 different kinds living virtually throughout the world; only the polar regions are completely without bats. The vast majority of bats feed on insects caught in flight. Known as insectivorous bats, most are fairly small in size and have only poor eyesight; but they have excellent echo-locating systems, frequently called sonar. Most bats set off at sunset to hunt, and although some fly for only a short time—then sleep until sunrise, when they again hunt for a short period—others fly through the night. They emit high-frequency squeaks and with their large, sensitive ears pick up the echoes which rebound off obstacles. This gives them a sound-picture of their surroundings which enables them not only to navigate safely in the dark but also to track and catch their food.

The greater horseshoe bat is one of a number of bats to have a peculiar fleshy fold of skin around the nostrils. These greatly concentrate the high-frequency sounds which are emitted through the nostrils; other bats emit these sounds through the mouth. The greater horseshoe bat often swoops down just above the ground to seize its prey, which includes dung-beetles, cockchafers and moths.

Just as there are birds which catch fish, so there are fishing bats. One little-known fish-eating bat lives in the Bay of California; another is the false

Opposite, top: The face that launched a thousand films—vampire bats at home, not in a Transylvanian castle but a South American cave.

Opposite, bottom: The wounded and debilitated bull shows the effect of vampire bat attacks.

Left: The vermilion flycatcher literally snatches its insect prey 'out of thin air' as they are both in flight.

vampire bat of India and South-East Asia, which also eats insects, frogs, birds and even other bats. A third kind lives in Central and South America and on some West Indian islands. Called the fish-eating or bulldog bat, it is thought to use echo-location to pinpoint fish as they break the surface of the water, and then uses its long, sharp claws as a gaff to impale the fish, which may measure up to 10 cm. This bat flies over fresh and salt water and sometimes hunts during the day, occasionally in the company of pelicans.

Central and South America are the homes of the true vampire bats, which enjoy nothing better than a meal of fresh, warm blood. Alighting gently on or near a sleeping animal, or even occasionally a human being, the vampire uses its razor-sharp teeth to pierce the skin so expertly that the victim does not wake.

The Reptiles

Long ago in the Earth's history there was an Age of Reptiles. This period lasted for about 100 million years and some of the reptiles, the dinosaurs, grew to amazing sizes—more than 20 m long and 50 tonnes in weight. These giants have long since become extinct, so now fossils, reconstructed giants and animated replicas in horror films, are all we have left. The reptiles that survive today rarely reach more than 6 m and the majority are much, much smaller. They all vary greatly in shape, size and habits but even so they are often the centre of attention because of their appearance and gruesome eating habits, and because, too, they sometimes kill man for food.

Snakes are often singled out as the cold-blooded killers of the reptile world, because they eat only live prey and always swallow it whole. To do this they have specially adapted teeth and jaws. All snakes have sharp, solid teeth, and usually many of them, with which the animal prey is seized. These teeth point slightly backwards and also serve to push the food down the throat, as snakes are unable to chew food or tear it into small pieces, as would a lion or eagle. Inside the stomach, juices are secreted that can digest everything except hair, horn and teeth. When all that can be digested by the snake has been dealt with, the indigestible pieces are brought up and ejected via the mouth.

In the wild each snake species has its own particular way of tracking down its animal prey. Some snakes are non-poisonous, such as the grass snakes, boa constrictors, anacondas and pythons. In the wild they are notably inoffensive when approached by human observers, but they do have about 100 teeth that can give a nasty bite. A snake tracks its prey by sight and scent. The forked tongue flicks out and picks up particles of matter in the air and on the ground. The scent of these is interpreted in the 'Jacobson's organ' in the roof of the snake's mouth. Constrictors, such as the boa, get their name from the way they kill their prey. The snake's teeth hold the prey firmly, and then the snake's body is thrown round the victim in a series of coils which are contracted or 'constricted'. With great strength the snake squeezes the victim's body until the heart stops beating. The prey can no longer breathe and dies of suffocation. The process is so swift that a small animal, such as a mouse, may be killed in seconds. Only if the prey is quite large and strong, or if the coils are incorrectly placed, is the struggle between snake and victim likely to be long. The remains of a leopard were discovered in the stomach of a 6 m Indian python, which shows how efficient constrictors can be in subduing formidable prey. The leopard had been able to inflict only insignificant wounds on its attacker. Examinations of animals that have been killed by constriction show little evidence of crushing. Bones such as ribs are sometimes fractured, but the prey is never squeezed into a pulp as many horror stories relate.

A snake's remarkable power of swallowing prey that is several times its own diameter is due to the special structure of its jaws. The two parts of the lower jaw are connected to the skull by a pair of lever-like bones that enable the mouth to be opened very wide. These two parts of the lower jaws also have some independence in movement. They can be widely separated when prey is being engulfed.

Opposite: The glistening muscular coils of the cascobel will squeeze the breath out of its prey.

Below: The African rock python can engulf prey such as a small wild pig, and then need not eat again for several weeks.

The giant of all constricting snakes is the anaconda that lives in northern South America. Although it is reported to reach about 10 m in length, this is much larger than most specimens. The anaconda is a snake of the numerous waterways of the Amazon Basin, feeding mainly on mammals and birds that live along the riverbanks. It will often drag its prey into the river to constrict it. When resting, this giant snake often uses the trees along the banks as a refuge. The female anaconda gives birth to more than 30 live young.

Another giant constrictor that may reach 10 m in length is the reticulated python of South-East Asia and the Philippines. There is an authenticated case of this snake eating a full-sized bear that would have weighed about 100 kg. However, records show that they do prefer smaller animals as victims. As the victim is swallowed, the stomach becomes distended and stretches the body skin. The snake lies for days quite motionless while the meal is digested. In the end a large ball of fur, teeth and other indigestible parts is disgorged—all that remains of its victim.

One of the best known species of constrictor is the boa constrictor which inhabits much of tropical America. It grows up to about 4 m in length, although the majority are 2 to 3 m long.

The extremely poisonous snakes are those that attack and kill their prey by biting it with long fangs which inject poison into the victim. Poison is ejected via the fangs, flowing down a groove in the back of each fang. The most poisonous snakes include cobras, kraits and mambas.

The Indian cobra and king cobra are two highly poisonous species that live in India. The 2 m Indian cobra is responsible for at least a quarter of all the snakebite deaths of humans in that country. It usually attacks at night, surprising people walking barefoot along tracks. They fail to see the cobra, which is well hidden in the dust and vegetation at the side of the path.

Yet a cobra does give good warning that it is about to attack. First it erects the front part of the body, at the same time flattening the neck by raising the long spines on its neck vertebrae. As the neck is flattened, characteristic markings that look like a pair of spectacles appear on the flattened neck—known as a hood. Then the cobra sways from side to side, which is probably how it measures the distance to its victim. Suddenly, at remarkable speed, the head shoots forwards and downwards and a strike is made. It is because of this behaviour, which gives good warning of the snake's intentions, that snake charmers can handle cobras easily.

It is the cobra that is often attacked and killed by the mongoose. The cobra is at a disadvantage because the mongoose is quick and agile, and darts here and there. The cobra cannot cope with the quick movements and has no time to focus accurately on a spot to attack. The mongoose also fluffs up its long fur which gives some protection if the cobra does manage to strike. The mongoose is nimble enough to get a grasp of the cobra's neck and kill it. There is also evidence that the mongoose has a high natural immunity to the venom of cobras.

The king cobra is also called the hamadryad. It is the largest and most dangerous of all poisonous snakes, and can grow to about 5 m.

In India an estimated 30,000 people die each year from the bite of a snake. Apart from the king and Indian cobra, other poisonous snakes responsible include the common krait, coral snake, Russell's viper and the saw-scaled viper.

The black-necked cobra of Africa is sometimes called the spitting cobra, as it has the habit of spitting its poison towards the eyes of its enemies. If the venom hits the eyes, it can momentarily blind and confuse the enemy. It causes harm only if there is an abrasion on the skin, but prompt washing with clean water will help save a person's sight if they have been hit.

The mambas are found only in Africa, where they live mainly in trees. They are extremely poisonous and attack with lightning speed and feroc-

Opposite, top, right: The black cobra. Opposite top, far right: The king cobra. Both among the deadliest of snakes, they show the front and rear of their distinctive hoods.

Opposite, bottom: The green mamba, camouflaged by its colouring among the jungle leaves, can strike like deadly lightning.

ity. If bitten it is said that a person has less than ten minutes to live. The venom produces weakness in the muscles and depresses the rate of breathing and the heartbeat.

The vipers and rattlesnakes belong to the same family. They have the same type of fangs and use them in the same way. The bones bearing the fangs can be swung forwards and upwards, the fangs moving with them. The fangs' tips have only to touch the victim because the venom or poison runs down a canal to the bevel-edged tip of each fang.

The common European viper or adder is the most widely distributed species, occurring throughout Europe, and central and northern Asia. It even lives within the Arctic circle in Scandinavia and is the only poisonous snake in Great Britain. It usually lives in dry places such as heaths and moorlands, and loves to sunbathe. It is active mainly at night, searching for rodents, lizards, birds, frogs and toads. Its bite is dangerous, and if surprised it attacks without warning.

There are many kinds of viper, with the Gaboon viper, rhinoceros viper and puff adder perhaps being the best known. The rhinoceros viper is so called because of the two raised scales at the tip of the snout. The puff adder, as its name suggests, blows itself up when alarmed by taking in air, so looking larger than it really is. The snake hisses vigorously as well.

Rattlesnakes, of which there are some 26 species, are found only in North America. The rattle at the end of the tail is formed by a series of loosely connected horny segments. When the animal moves, these segments make a noise like a baby's rattle. Every time the rattlesnake sheds its skin, another segment is added to the tail. Although there is a segment added each time the snake moults, which should enable one to count how many moults the snake has made, this is not the case, as the horny tail or rattle is often damaged and segments are lost through wear and tear. The most dangerous and well-known of rattlesnakes is the diamondback of Florida and Georgia. It gets its name from the diamond markings on its back.

Opposite: The African puff adder, among other snakes, may hiss as a warning. Opposite, inset: The 'heat pits' on the head of the horned viper allow it to detect warm-blooded prey at a distance.

Below: The diamondback rattlesnake at least has the grace to warn of its intentions by rattling its tail, before it strikes.

Crocodiles and other members of their group, including alligators, caiman and gharials, have an elongated body with strong legs. They are the closest living reptiles to the enormous dinosaurs of the Age of Reptiles. All are amphibious in habit and dangerous to any living thing that enters their domain. Their eyes, nostrils and ears are placed at the top of the head, enabling the animal to use these organs while the rest of its body is submerged. This allows them to drift slowly downstream within striking distance of a chosen victim.

Their jaws are large, long and strong, with an excellent set of powerful teeth. All the teeth are the same shape, like small pointed cones, each set in a socket. The teeth can certainly grip a victim, but they are unable to slice or bite chunks out of the prey. When a crocodile grasps a victim, the animal is often dragged beneath the water to drown. Then the crocodile twists its whole body around, pulling at the carcass until a piece of flesh is ripped off. No water enters the nose or lungs while this is happening, as all members of the crocodile group have a palate that separates the mouth from the nose passages and the lung passages.

Man-eating crocodiles are still found today, although very large specimens of more than 6 m are quite rare. This is because so many crocodiles and alligators have been killed in the past for their valuable skins which are used in the leather industry. There are still reports of huge specimens surviving in remote areas. In 1978 in the far north of Queensland, Australia, an estuarine or salt-water crocodile attacked a 4 m long aluminium boat powered by an outboard motor. The two men in the boat were thrown into the river and safely reached the shore. Later they retrieved their boat and found the petrol tank and motor sliced in two, and the boat severely dented. A few days later a salt-water crocodile was seen on the bank and estimated at about 7·5 m. As crocodiles are protected in Australia people in the area are very wary. This species of crocodile is known to be dangerous to man, being fierce and easily aroused.

Perhaps the strangest-looking member of the crocodile group is the Indian gavial or gharial which lives in the waters of the Ganges, Mahanadi, Brahmaputra and Indus river basins. It has a long, rod-like snout that widens into a bulbous knob at the nostrils. It feeds almost entirely on fish and although it can give a painful bite, it is not dangerous to humans.

Tortoises, turtles and terrapins are rather slow-moving reptiles that usually feed on fruit, vegetables and plants. There are one or two that have strange eating habits and are strictly carnivorous. The freshwater pond tortoise feeds on fish, frogs, insects, worms, snails and small shellfish, but will also consume small mice and other rodents as well as young birds if it gets the chance. At only 30 cm in length, however, it is not a threat to humans!

The most aggressive member of the tortoise group is without doubt the alligator snapping turtle which is found in the USA. It is well named because a full grown snapping turtle can severely damage a man's hand if carelessly handled. It causes the injury with its strong, hooked beak.

The alligator snapping turtle spends most of its life in muddy ponds, lakes or rivers. Here it lies in wait for its prey, half buried in the mud and camouflaged by the algae and weeds growing from its flattened shell. From this hiding place the alligator snapping turtle lures small fish into its mouth by a remarkable trick. Its tongue is

Opposite, top: The tongue-tip in the mouth of the alligator snapping turtle looks like a wriggling worm, and lures fish prey into the deadly jaws.

Opposite, bottom: Although designed for water life, the alligator can move surprisingly quickly on land.

Below: The Nile crocodile demonstrates jaws that can tear apart large prey.

forked and the two branches are pinkish, fat and worm-like. The turtle moves its tongue, making the 'worms' wriggle, and small fish are attracted to this apparent food. Then they are promptly snapped up. This turtle is also fast enough to chase and catch larger prey such as ducklings.

Among the 2,500 or so different kinds of lizard there are few killers. The most ferocious is an incredible 3 m monitor lizard. This is the Komodo dragon, which lives on certain small islands in South-East Asia, particularly Komodo Island. It feeds on young deer, wild pigs and occasionally attacks wild horses. It is such a deadly killer that it has been known to attack, kill and eat its own kind, as well as devouring any dead bodies of other animals it comes across.

It is perhaps surprising that there are only two species of lizard that are poisonous. These are found only in the deserts of Arizona, Nevada and Utah in the USA and in Mexico. They are called the gila monster and the beaded lizard. Their scales look like beads and are many-coloured, with designs of yellow to orange-red on a dark-brown (almost black) background. They differ from snakes in that the venom is secreted by a gland in the lower jaw. The teeth make an open wound in the prey and the venom, mixed with the saliva of the lizard, enters it. The bite is rarely lethal to humans.

The strangest killing technique among the lizards is seen in the 80 or so kinds of chameleon which live in Africa and Madagascar. These tree-dwelling creatures have eyes that move independently, giving separate views that are co-ordinated in the chame-

Opposite, top: The gecko often frequents human homes in its tropical habitat.

Opposite, bottom: The chameleon has the disturbing ability to move its eyes in two directions at once.

Below: Villain of many a western film, the gila monster has a bite as poisonous as that of many snakes.

leon's brain into an all-round picture. This binocular vision enables the reptile to estimate distances, such as prey distance, accurately.

When the distance of a chosen victim has been judged the chameleon gets its club-shaped tongue ready. When at rest the chameleon's tongue is contracted inside the mouth. When the reptile is about to strike at an insect it aims its head, opens its mouth, brings its tongue slowly forwards to the front of the jaws, then suddenly shoots the tongue out by a complicated action of special muscles. The tongue can extend until it is as long as the chameleon's body. The tongue tip is sticky and has some muscular grasping ability. As soon as the prey is caught the tongue is pulled back into the mouth at a slower rate. Locusts are about the biggest prey caught.

Insects, Spiders and Plants

The millions upon millions of different insects that live all around the world are eaten by many animals. There are also many insects that wage battle and kill other insects for food.

In freshwater ponds and lakes, several insect hunters live on other water-dwelling animals. The giant water bug hides motionless in water weeds waiting for its chance to strike. When its victim comes close the bug attacks, grasping the creature with its front legs until its piercing beak can be plunged into the victim. This bug will attack tadpoles, larvae of other insects, and even fish up to twice its own size. When the beak is inserted, in the same way a syringe is used to inject a liquid into a human, the bug pumps a type of digestive juice down its beak into the victim. This dissolves the tissues which are then sucked back in liquid form. The victim does not struggle for long, because it is quickly paralysed and poisoned by the injected juice.

On land the assassin bugs are some of the most expert of insect hunters. There are more than 2,500 species throughout the world. One kind of assassin bug captures bees. It does this by entangling the bee in the strong bristles on its legs. Some assassin bugs run after their victims and pounce, while others spring out from hiding. The victims are held by sticky, oily, hairy pads on the bug's legs. The victims are poisoned and have their body tissues turned into liquid by the same method that is used by the water bug.

A formidable, well-known insect that preys on insects is the praying mantis. The word 'mantis' comes from a Greek word which means 'priest' or 'soothsayer'. This name is applied to the mantis because when it is resting or lying in wait for a victim, it assumes a prayer-like attitude: the head and front part of the body are held up, with the long, strong, grasping legs folded as though the insect is in prayer.

Mantids are masters of disguise. Most of the 1,800 species that live in the tropics and warmer parts of the world are beautifully camouflaged to match their surroundings. Some mantids even resemble flowers, attracting flower-loving insects such as bees and butterflies which soon meet their doom. All the mantids are carnivorous and often cannibalistic, the larger attacking the smaller. The female, in fact, will often eat the male while he is actually mating with her.

Mantids seize their prey with their spiny forelegs. When shot out from the folded resting position, these forelegs can reach almost the same length as the mantid's body. The forelegs grasp the victim tightly and draw it to the mouth, where the strong jaws or mandibles cut the prey into small bits for swallowing.

Among the most attractive and best loved of the beetles are the ladybirds or ladybugs. There are various bright colours and patterns among the 5,000 species found living in the world. Most are welcomed by the gardener and farmer because they prey on aphids or greenfly, scale insects and other smaller insects that are pests to crops and plants. One species that lives in Australia was introduced into California, USA, to help control a scale insect pest that was destroying orange, lemon and grapefruit crops.

The ant lions are neither ants nor lions. They are the larvae, or young, of adult insects that look very much like dragonflies. The fat but flat-bodied larvae grow up to 2·5 cm long. With their long, spreading jaws they dig large, conical pits in loose sand or fine soil. Here they lie in wait. At the bottom of the pits the larvae bury themselves leaving only their jaws exposed. The jaws seize any ant or other small insect that tumbles or slides down the steep, sandy walls of the pit. The victims are seized, their bodies pierced and drained dry, and their empty body shells discarded.

All spiders are predatory, with their jaws modified to form poison fangs for killing their prey. The venom of a few

Opposite: Perhaps the most horrific of spiders, the hairy tarantula has a bite which kills small prey and can make humans very ill.

spiders, such as the black widow or the tarantula, is dangerous to man. The tarantula, bird-eating, and wolf spiders are the best known hunters in the world of spiders.

The bird-eating spider is a night hunter, living in Central and South America. This spider does not build a web like most of its relatives. With its legs, which in some species spread 18 cm or more, it runs down its prey or seizes it after a sudden silent dash. As well as insects it will take small mammals such as mice and sleeping hummingbirds. Taking birds as prey has given this spider its common name.

The wolf spider also runs down its prey, and this behaviour, likened to a wolf hunting its victim, has given this medium-sized spider its name. It lives mainly among leaf litter. At night, or in overcast conditions, it leaves the shelter of its small burrow to hunt. The tarantula of southern Europe is a wolf spider.

The tarantula's name comes from the town of Taranto in southern Italy. Legend has it that its bite was fatal to humans unless the victim danced until exhausted. During this dance, known as the 'tarantella', all the poison would be sweated from the system. The legend was in existence before Columbus discovered America. When the bird-eating spiders were discovered in America they, too, were called tarantulas, so much confusion occurs when talking about these deadly spiders.

The garden or cross spider is a familiar spider which is harmless to humans—as are its relatives, the orb spiders. These spiders spin characteristic spiral, silken webs and sit at the centre, waiting for an insect to get caught in the sticky drops on the spiral threads. When an insect touches the web, the vibrations it sets up inform the spider that a meal awaits. It rushes to the victim, jabs its poison fangs into the struggling prey, and

Below: The web of a garden spider, sparkling with dew, looks more like a beautiful necklace than a trap.

shrouds it with silk. The spider then eats its victim at leisure, and quickly repairs any damage done to its web.

Surprisingly enough, there are even a few plants that feed on insect prey. They live in poor soil where they cannot obtain enough nitrogen, so they take this vital chemical from living prey. They are called insectivorous plants, and have some wonderful methods of trapping their victims. Those that can be found growing wild in Britain are the butterwort, sundew and bladderwort. But the best-known examples of insectivorous plants, found in tropical countries, are probably the Venus flytrap and the pitcher-plants. The Venus flytrap catches insects with its leaves. The leaves, arranged in a circle or rosette, have two lobes on either side of the midrib. On the leaf edges are long, firm spikes. The surface of each leaf bears sensitive bristles. If an insect alights on the leaf surface and touches the bristles, the leaf lobes move suddenly towards each other and the long spikes intertwine to form a cage in which the insect is trapped. Glands in the leaves begin to give off digestive enzymes which break down the protein in the trapped creature. The liquid protein is absorbed by the plant and the Venus flytrap receives its extra nitrogen.

The pitcher-plants are probably the most remarkable insectivorous plants. Their leaves are modified to form hollow pitchers. The rim of a pitcher is firm and shiny and curves inwards. The outside of the pitcher is usually brightly coloured, ranging, in different species, from bright red through orange to yellow. The stem of the plant and the pitcher give off a sweet, honey-like substance. All these things attract insects, which try to get inside the pitcher to obtain the nectar. In doing so they slip on the shiny, smooth rim and fall to the bottom. Here a protein-digesting liquid breaks down the insects' proteins and absorbs the nitrogen. Even if insects try to climb out of the liquid, they find a ring of hairs all pointing downwards to prevent their escape. Exhausted, they eventually fall down and drown.

Left: At any second the fly may trigger the jaws of the Venus fly-trap and enclose itself in a death cell.

Below: The graceful pitcher-plant has a lid that snaps down to keep in prey while it is digested by the plant.

Freshwater Hunters

The waters of the world are home to a great number of hunters, each adapted to survive in its own individual way. In the freshwater areas of the world there are various habitats, or possible different kinds of aquatic homes, for predatory animals to hunt in. Rivers, lakes, swift-running streams, stagnant bogs—all have their own underwater hunters.

The majority of freshwater hunters are fish. These usually hunt fish smaller than themselves, other water-dwelling animals such as frogs, newts and toads, or soft-bodied animals such as worms.

There are a few specialist fish that have extremely interesting methods of catching their food. One such fish is the archer-fish of tropical South-East Asia and northern Australia. This fish varies its menu to include animals that do not live in the water where it swims. It is able to shoot down an insect that is flying or resting on leaves above the surface of the water. To do this, the archer-fish squirts a jet of water from its mouth. The jets are fired in rapid succession. The fish usually manages to hit an insect which drops on to the surface of the water, where

Opposite: A harvest mouse makes an unusual meal for a toad, which usually eats insects or worms.

Below: A pike has no qualms about eating another of its own kind.

Left: The freshwater perch hunts prey such as this water beetle larva in rivers and ponds. The larva is itself a fierce predator of smaller water animals.

Inset: The archer fish is a marksman of the animal world, shooting a jet of water to knock insects into its reach.

the archer-fish rapidly snaps it up. Large specimens of archer-fish are about 30 cm long and can hit insects more than 1 m away.

The climbing perch of South-East Asia is another fish that has evolved an amazing method of feeding and hunting. It is able to breathe oxygen in the air, as well as extracting oxygen from the water through its gills. It is also able to use its gill covers and lower fins as primitive limbs, enabling it to leave the water to hunt on the banks for a variety of small land-living animals.

There are many voracious freshwater fish that hunt and kill animals sharing their own watery world. Piranhas are probably the most famous for their voracity. They live in the rivers of tropical South America, usually in shoals which may number hundreds. Most of the time piranhas feed on smaller fish, such as their relatives, the characins. It is usually only by accident that they feed on larger animals. However, they can deal with animals such as the capybara, the world's largest rodent, which lives on the forest riverbanks. Even humans foolish enough to swim in piranha infested rivers are liable to be attacked. Many villagers living by such rivers have suffered bitten feet and hands, sometimes even losing a finger or toe. The piranha's teeth are large, flat and triangular, with razor-sharp edges, and the jaws are very powerful so that the fish can chop pieces of flesh from an animal almost without it noticing. Piranhas attack a large animal such as a horse in such great numbers that the victim is soon overcome. Because there may be thousands in the shoal devouring the animal, it is stripped of its flesh in a very short time. A capybara of 55 kg was stripped of its flesh in a few minutes.

Another famous killer living in South American rivers—especially the Amazon system—is the electric eel. This fish lives in muddy, slow-moving waters where sight does not help any hunter. The eel overcomes this by sending out small electrical impulses through the water to locate its prey. Any obstacle or prey within the electric field disrupts the impulses, and from the signals it gets back the eel can distinguish whether the object is edible, such as a fish, frog or larger creature, or just a rock. If it wishes to feed, it emits a powerful electric shock which stuns or kills its victim. The shock may be up to 550 volts and is discharged from disc-like cells which are specially-adapted muscle cells.

There are three different families of electric fish that live in fresh water: the South American electric eels and their relatives the knife-fish; the African snout fish; and the African electric catfish.

The African electric catfish ranges through the waters of Central Africa and down the Nile Valley. A large adult some 1·2 m long and weighing 23 kg can discharge as much as 100 volts. This slow, lazy fish uses its electric power to find its way about, to stun enemies, and to kill smaller fish to eat.

The most efficient fish killer of the rivers and lakes of the northern hemisphere is undoubtedly the pike. It has a broad, duck-like mouth and an array of needle-sharp teeth. It feeds mainly on fish, but scientists that have studied its stomach contents find that the pike will also take any frogs, small birds such as ducklings, and small mammals such as water voles, that come within range of its huge jaws. The pike may grow to more than 1·2 m long. It hunts by lurking motionless among water plants, waiting patiently for any unsuspecting and suitable prey to come within reach of its jaws.

One of the pike's favourite prey is the three-spined stickleback. This small fish is itself carnivorous, but it eats only small animals such as worms, and insect larvae. The three-spined stickleback has an efficient defence that sometimes saves it from the hungry pike. If the pike engulfs a three-spined stickleback, the small fish immediately raises its spines. These prick the pike's throat or mouth and prevent the stickleback from being swallowed. Often the pike has to spit out the stickleback and find another meal.

Opposite, top, right: The killing abilities of the piranha have inspired legends in its native South America.

Opposite, top, far right: The larva of the dragonfly, living in ponds and streams, has a large hinged jaw with which to catch its prey.

Opposite, bottom: The electric catfish, seen here with its young, is a lazy hunter emitting electric shocks to stun or kill its prey of smaller fish.

Killers of the Deep

However peaceful the sea might appear, beneath its surface a terrible battle constantly rages. There is a strange and frightening world beneath the sea: speed and cunning are all that really count. The greater the depth, the fewer living creatures exist there; and most of those are hunters or scavengers simply because the absence of light means there is little, if any, living vegetation. So 'kill or be killed' is the law that most sea creatures live and die by.

Nearer the water surface the pattern of life is more like that on land. Here, large carnivorous creatures such as sharks, seals and dolphins are at the head of a food chain that starts with microscopic plant and animal life, with shoaling fish forming the main part.

One of the most terrible animals roaming the high seas on its ceaseless quest for prey is the great white shark, also known as 'white death'. To describe it as rapacious or ferocious is somehow not sufficient. Measuring 6 to 7·5 m and weighing half a tonne, the great white shark belongs to a group of fish which possess no swim-bladder (a kind of air-filled buoyancy bag) and therefore have to keep swimming in order not to sink. These sharks are simply hunting and eating machines, guided by a remarkable sense system which is sensitive to the faintest vibrations and smells. Like other sharks, the great white shark can detect blood in the water at a concentration of only a few drops per million, and when it finds an injured creature—perhaps another shark, a fish or seal, or even a luckless human swimmer—it will slash into the prey with razor-sharp teeth in a feeding frenzy. No time is wasted on chewing—the shark neatly cuts off huge chunks and swallows them whole.

Living at much greater depths than these sharks is a still more sinister animal: the giant squid. No one knows for sure how big the giant squid grows, because the largest ones ever found (15 to 18 m long) were discovered in the stomachs of sperm whales, which themselves rarely exceed 18 m. As whales need to surface occasionally to breathe, this would put them at a serious disadvantage if locked in mortal combat with an equally large creature which never needs to surface. A squid longer than 18 m would be more than a match for the biggest sperm whale, and so evidence of its existence might never be seen. Bites and sucker marks more than 10 cm in diameter on sperm whales, bear witness to terrible encounters, but ones which presumably the whales won.

Sperm whales probably only encounter giant squid by chance. The echo-sounding navigation system which all whales use normally helps the sperm whale to locate its diet of smaller squid and cuttle-fish. To find their food they may possibly descend to 3,000 m, and can stay submerged for an hour or more.

Related to the sperm whale and the other predatory toothed whales are the great baleen or whalebone whales, a group that includes the blue whale—the greatest animal that has ever lived on this planet. Instead of teeth these whales have a row of fibrous plates suspended from the roof of the mouth. The whales open their mouths to trap the 'soup' of animal plankton on which they feed; then they close their jaws, push the water out through the baleen plates, and eat the filtered plankton left in the mouth.

Opposite: Despite its fearsome reputation, the killer whale is an intelligent and amiable creature in captivity.

Opposite, inset: Eternally on the look-out for prey, the white-tip shark prowls on the fringes of a coral reef.

Left: The moray eel is justly feared by divers, for it lurks in rock crannies waiting to attack with its needle-sharp teeth.

Opposite, top: The anglerfish lies on the sea bed waiting for an unwary fish to take his 'lure'.

Opposite, bottom: Looking like a strange bird, the spotted whip ray cruises through tropical waters.

Right: Like many oceanic fish, barracuda are streamlined for speed.

Below: The leopard shark is spotted like its land-living namesake.

Plankton is the 'animal pasture' of the seas, and browsing on it are great shoals of fish such as herring. Preying in turn on these fish are medium-sized and large sea predators, from barracuda and seals to tuna, turtles and the sharks.

Another important group of predators with a highly specialized hunting technique are the electric rays. They have disc-shaped bodies with wing-like flapping fins extending from the sides of the head along the body. They are found in all tropical waters, and venture to a depth of 1,000 m.

Electric rays 'pounce' on their prey, wrap their cloak-like fins around it, and stun it by an electric shock of up to 20 volts from organs situated on both sides of the body, and controlled by nerves in a special part of the brain.

Unlike the sharks and rays, which have cartilaginous skeletons, the most important group of fish have true bony skeletons. This group includes thousands of species, from swordfish to tiny cleaner wrasse. There are many specialist hunters among them. The barracuda is a particularly ferocious predator, growing to 2·5 m long and weighing 45 kg. It has a slim body and powerful jaws armed with sharp teeth. It lives in warm waters off the American coast and around the Caribbean Sea.

Swordfish, such as the marlin, are also bony fish. They have a rapier-like bill which helps them cut through the water. They reach speeds of 80 kmph, making them among the fastest of all swimmers. Although they use their swords for striking to both sides in a shoal of fish to injure as many as possible, there is evidence that they do actually impale prey as well. The sword is certainly capable of an extraordinary thrust when being propelled at these high speeds, and there are reports of marlin swords being driven through ship's timber 56 cm thick.

Angler fish have a highly specialized and unique form of hunting. The first ray of the spiny dorsal fin curves forward and has a luminous or wriggly tip, like a fishing rod with a bait. This dangles in front of its enormous jaws and attracts unwary victims—which are often almost its own size. The unsuspecting victim approaches the lure in curiosity, but as soon as it is close enough, the huge needle-toothed jaws of the angler fish snap up the prey.

Dolphins and seals are both sea-living mammals and are, to a certain extent, competitors. Both have fish as a staple part of their diet. Dolphins are as aquatic as the fish they prey on apart from their need to breathe air at the surface. Seals, on the other hand, must return to dry land in order to breed, and to moult their thick coats.

Seals hunt as individuals, while dolphins hunt in well-organized groups, herding shoals of fish together and preventing their escape. People who have watched captive dolphins will know something of their astonishing physical and mental abilities. The echo-location or 'sonar' they use to find fish and navigate in murky water is so effective that a blindfolded dolphin can speedily cross a pool latticed with fine wires and pick up a fish thrown in the far end, without touching one wire.

Seals, such as the grey seals, which are familiar around the coasts of north-

Below: The dolphin and sea lion (opposite,) may seem to be laughing with their human friends, but their sharp teeth betray their role as hunters.

Right: Seals are efficient hunters of fish shoals.

Opposite, top, right: In the Antarctic the leopard seal may prey on the cubs of other seals (opposite, top, far right).

Opposite, bottom: None, however, is a match for their natural enemy, the killer whale.

ern Europe, and the eared seals or sea-lions (which include the fur seals), rely on their speed and manoeuvrability to catch fish. They are aided by their whiskers which are sensitive to the slightest changes in water pressure and so alert the seal to a fish swimming nearby. Seals home in on these vibrations in much the same way as dolphins use echo-location. The leopard seal of the Antarctic, richly deserving its name, is one of the most ferocious of killers. As well as fish it will take other seals and penguins—it will even pursue them on to ice floes—and makes short work of its prey with its long, sharp teeth.

The killer whale has a fearsome reputation which is reflected in its name. It feeds mainly on fish and squid, but it is also an efficient hunter of dolphins, seals and penguins. One killer whale caught in the Bering Sea was found to have the remains of 32 seals in its stomach; another, 13 dolphins and 14 seals. The prey is sometimes swallowed whole, as proved by the discovery of a complete 3 m-long dolphin in a killer whale's stomach. Even the great baleen whales are not safe, and schools of killers will single out one from a herd (probably a young or sickly specimen) and pursue it relentlessly—some hanging on to its tail and fins while others dart at the corners of its mouth to seek its tongue—the greatest delicacy.